BLACK & WHITE WORLD

BLACK & WHITE WORLD

EDITORIAL CARTOONS

BY

Cox & Forkum

COX & FORKUM

Nashville, Tennessee

ISBN 0-9724569-0-2

First printing October 2002

Printed in the United States

Published by
COX & FORKUM
1121 Airport Center Drive
Nashville, TN 37214
(615) 843-0697

Book design by Allen Forkum
Illustrations by John Cox

contents

acknowledgments

The authors wish to thank Robert and Sherri Tracinski
for publishing many of these cartoons under the auspices
of *The Intellectual Activist*.

introduction

In September of 2001, Allen Forkum sent me the first Cox & Forkum cartoon I ever saw, "Weight of the World" (70). That first cartoon was enough to convince me that these guys had talent. It made a good point, did so in an original way, and made me laugh. The phrase attributed to the teacher—"boiling rain will scald all the baby animals"—was the part that got me the most. Its comic exaggeration perfectly captures the absurdity of today's environmental hysterias, but it also poignantly exposes the way environmentalists exploit a child's love of animals. It succeeded at a political cartoonist's most difficult task: making a serious point, but with a touch of humor.

For years, I had been looking for a cartoonist who would match the perspective of my magazine, *The Intellectual Activist*. I tried, briefly, publishing the work of a conservative syndicated cartoonist, but I found it a stretch. *TIA*'s outlook is not "conservative"; we do not look backward and attempt to preserve traditional values for their own sake. *TIA* advocates basic principles—reason, individualism, secularism, individual rights and capitalism—that are still radical, unorthodox and "politically incorrect" today. Those principles obviously put us at odds with the subjectivism and socialism of the left; but they also put us at odds with the religious and pragmatist tendencies of the right.

What impressed me most, however, was not just that Allen and John shared *TIA*'s perspective. It was the fact that they expressed their viewpoint in creative ways, offering new observations and striking

images. Who else would have thought of sending the Taliban to the Arctic National Wildlife Refuge (94)? (Come to think of it, maybe that's a better spot than sunny Guantanamo.) And they always pay attention to the small details that add an extra little zing. For example, don't miss the menu in "Clones" (64).

Editorial cartoons are more than just humorous frivolities; they have a more important purpose than just getting a chuckle. They are indispensable in helping readers concretize the meaning of world events. A written editorial can explore new ideas, project the logical consequences of a course of action, or analyze the deeper meaning of widely held notions. But it does so through long explanations, a string of abstractions that do not have the immediate power of visual reality. That's where the cartoonist comes in. He takes the kind of conclusions an editorialist expresses in words and projects them in a visual form—exaggerating real events, setting familiar characters in an unfamiliar setting, or placing side by side the two halves of a contradiction our political leaders desperately try to keep separated.

The cartoonist creates a visual symbol that captures, with an immediate, memorable impact, the underlying meaning of the day's headlines. Want an image to capture the inadequacy of relying solely on defensive "homeland security" measures? Imagine President Bush placing the nation's security in the quaking hands of Barney Fife (21). Want a symbol of the State Department's appeasement of

Arab fanatics? Picture Colin Powell in a turban (13). And Saddam Hussein as a cockroach (19)—well, that speaks for itself.

In this collection, those who are already familiar with Cox & Forkum's cartoons will be able to revisit some old favorites and discover some terrific pieces that have never before seen print. They will also, I think, gain a new appreciation by seeing all of the cartoons in one place and having the benefit of Allen's and John's illuminating commentaries. I particularly enjoyed hearing John talk about these cartoons from the artist's perspective, explaining the visual cues he uses to convey his message.

For those who have never seen these cartoons before—you're in for a visual and intellectual treat: John's arresting images and Allen's pungent wit. I feel fortunate to have been the first to see these cartoons and to have had the opportunity to get in on the beginning of what I think will be a very successful partnership.

That joy of discovery will now be yours.

Robert W. Tracinski
Editor & Publisher
The Intellectual Activist
www.IntellectualActivist.com

preface

This book features Cox & Forkum editorial cartoons created between September 2001 and September 2002. Many of them have never before been published. Cartoons previously published in *The Intellectual Activist*, on its Web site and in AutoGraphic's *Automotive Report* publications are marked with an asterisk (*) by the title.

Commentaries by Allen Forkum and John Cox begin each chapter with the aim of providing context and creative insight.[†]

The title, *Black & White World*, alludes to both the use of pen-and-ink drawings and the advocacy of absolute moral principles. Many of these cartoons were inspired by Objectivism, which is the philosophy of Ayn Rand. For authoritative presentations of her philosophy, readers are referred to her writings, particularly the novels *The Fountainhead* and *Atlas Shrugged*, and the non-fiction books *The Virtue of Selfishness* and *Capitalism: The Unknown Ideal.*

Furthermore, editorial cartoons by their nature tend to be negative criticism that merely imply positive answers. For a full analysis of issues raised here, readers are encouraged to check out the editorials listed in the References section, which include a number of entries from the weekly columns of Robert W. Tracinski (www.IntellectualActivist.com) and op-ed releases from The Ayn Rand Institute (www.aynrand.org).

[†] *In commentaries throughout this book, numbers in parenthesis refer to a cartoon's page number. Footnote numbers correspond to the References section in the back of the book, which is a list of relevant documents, news articles and editorials.*

BLACK
&WHITE
WORLD

OSAMA BIN LADEN

FORKUM: After the atrocities of Sept. 11, 2001, Osama bin Laden became a natural target for cartoons as well as cruise missiles. He deserved it sooner. Not only had he already committed terror attacks against America, he had publicly *declared war* on us. Our government's response? A mere criminal indictment against him.

On Sept. 20, 2001, President Bush proclaimed that we would "bring justice to our enemies" but that Americans should expect a "lengthy campaign."[1] I for one thought we had kept bin Laden waiting long enough (facing page).

When Bush rightly called the Sept. 11 terrorists "cowardly," one commentator insisted they were brave for committing suicide in the attacks.[2] But no matter how far one stretches the concept of bravery, it will never include those who stalk and murder defenseless civilians of a free country. If not dead already, bin Laden is hiding in a dark hole somewhere in the middle of Milesofsandistan (4). What's brave about that?

The truth is that *fear* is a primary motive of Islamic terrorists. They fear the power, influence and widespread love of secular Western culture (10). They fear the political and economic freedom that leads to our prosperity and might. They fear *us* and so lash out in the only way possible for irrational religious fanatics—with brute force.

We made few cartoons about bin Laden because, not only was he not the main enemy, we figured he wouldn't be in the picture very long.

I thank our brave armed forces for that.

COX: An early cartoon of ours, "Swift Justice" (facing page), is still one of my favorites. We wanted to avoid a mere physical caricature of Osama bin Laden and go for his character. Elusive, craven, creepy and essentially weak, he had the makings for a rat. Contrasted with the decisive and heroic eagle (drawn more realistically than the rat), the America Fights Back vibe is accomplished.

My approach of contrasting goofy exaggeration with realistic drama captured what we set out to do with these pieces: showcase pointed, principled commentary with zingy, black-and-white artwork. And every once in a while go for a good laugh.

"Rosie '01" (6) was a fun attempt at updating an icon. Norman Rockwell created "Rosie the Riveter" to show how women were an important part of the '40s war effort. Not only did this seem like a relevant contemporary idea, but it stands in stark contrast to Islamic ideals of women.

So I whipped out my book of Rockwell paintings and brought Rosie back, kicking tail and putting bin Laden in his place.

Ever wonder why Rosie looks so masculine? The original Rosie was an update herself. Rockwell used Michelangelo's "Isaiah" from the Sistine Chapel as a reference.

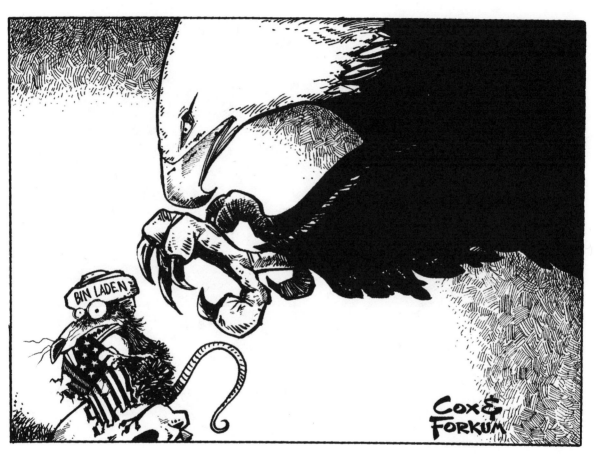

Swift Justice* / Oct. 8, 2001

Oct. 6, 2001

Oct. 13, 2001

Rosie '01 / Nov. 26, 2001

Man of the Year* / Jan. 3, 2002

WAR ON TERRORISM

FORKUM: The first attempts to undermine America's resolve to wage war came from the (supposed) pacifists, who demanded that the attacks be treated as crimes and not acts of war. This would have meant bringing justice merely to those directly involved, most of whom conveniently committed suicide in the attacks. This approach, like chopping off only one head of the mythical Hydra (facing page), would have left intact the *source* of the danger: terrorist-sponsoring states.

So I found it very heartening when President Bush declared, "From this day forward, any nation that continues to harbor or support terrorism will be regarded by the United States as a hostile regime."[1]

Likewise, I found it heartbreaking when this so-called Bush Doctrine and the War on Terrorism were gradually made impotent by Bush's compromises on such issues as:

— a coalition with tyrannical states (13);
— civilians in enemy territory (11, 12);
— Palestinian statehood (45); and
— the terrorism of Yasser Arafat (48).

Blame for these capitulations rests partly on the shoulders of Secretary of State Colin "Please Don't Hate Us" Powell (23). But he can be fired.[3]

It reached the point where our government seemed more concerned with creating a veneer of "homeland" security than dealing with the real threats from abroad (22).

COX: The war cartoons had all the makings of some of my most energetic work. The challenge of conveying conflict, patriotism, perseverance and justice—all with the backdrop of deadly action—was definitely right in my wheelhouse.

"Hydra" (facing page) and "Let Freedom Ring" (20) make use of wonderfully visual metaphors. I really enjoy these kinds of cartoons because they put a premium on intensity and inventiveness.

In "Hydra," I wanted to show a strong Uncle Sam. Contemporary cartoons often show him as an ineffectual old man beaten down by conflicting feelings of guilt and power. But why not show Uncle Sam as a well-built, vibrant symbol of patriotic resolve and steadfast ideals? Why not show him as he *ought* to be? This Uncle Sam could easily defeat the Hydra—if only he chooses to.

The look of the Hydra was inspired by Ray Harryhausen's creation for the movie *Jason and the Argonauts*.

"Let Freedom Ring" took an old American icon and gave it new life. It already had weight and symbolic import. But what can it *do*? Well, it could put a big hurt on someone if it fell from a few hundred feet. Enter our enemy and—WHANG!—the Liberty Bell becomes a symbolic weapon of reprisal. I really enjoyed trying to show the sheer mass and age of such a well-known icon and still get across Allen's sense of whimsy.

Hydra* / Sept. 30, 2001

Culture War* / Oct. 5, 2001

Civilians* / Oct. 14, 2001

Nov. 6, 2001

Coalition* / Nov. 12, 2001

Nov. 23, 2001

Nov. 27, 2001

Beginning of the End* / Nov. 29, 2001

Walker* / Dec, 17, 2001

POW?* / Jan. 29, 2002

Cockroach* / Feb. 18, 2002

Let Freedom Ring* / June 25, 2002

The Great White Lie / July 15, 2002

Evasion, U.S.A. / July 17, 2002

To The Rescue? / Aug. 6, 2002

Trash Talk* / Aug. 9, 2002

Saddam's Shell Game* / Aug. 12, 2002

CONFRONTING TERRORISM...

Confronting Terrorism* / Sept. 8, 2002

Anger Management / Sept. 8, 2002

Domino Effect / Sept. 9, 2002

UNfree / Sept. 14, 2002

ISLAMISM

FORKUM: President Bush assured us that Islam had been "hijacked" by the Sept. 11 terrorists[1], and obviously millions of Muslims do live peacefully among others. But just as obviously there are fanatics who want to force their interpretations of Islam on us (33). The difference? The militants—Islamists—use terror as a means to an end: the establishment of totalitarian Islamic states.[4]

As former Israeli Prime Minister Benjamin Netanyahu observed: "It is not merely that the goals of terrorists do not justify the means they use. It is that the means that they choose tell you what their real goals are, because those who target the innocent will never protect freedom and human rights."[5]

For Islamists, the use of force replaces discourse. Dogmatic faith replaces logic and reason. Self-sacrificial suffering replaces the pursuit of happiness. The "next world" replaces this world. Ultimately, death itself becomes a goal[6] (facing page). As one of bin Laden's spokesmen put it: "There are thousands of the Islamic nation's youths who are eager to die just as the Americans are eager to live."[7]

Until fundamentalist Islam, like other religions, is tamed by Western values such as individual rights, secularism and the rule of law, more suicide murderers and religious tyrannies are inevitable (34). I hope that, as the more secular Muslims point out the distinction between themselves and Islamists, they will also point out the necessity of separating church and state (41).

COX: Does a cartoon *have* to be funny? Or can it be macabre? And if so, how far into the macabre can it properly go to make a point? I can honestly say that "Death Worshippers" (facing page) tested me on those very questions.

To portray Islamists' reverence for death and destruction, Allen came up with the idea of parodying the movie poster for *Gone With the Wind*. The intensity of feeling between Gable and Leigh seemed like a good start, but I must admit that I had to be dragged kicking and screaming to draw it. I prefer drawing lighthearted images, and just the thought of this one gave me some serious willies. I told Allen, "This is not funny." He replied, "Exactly."

I came to understand the potential impact of illustrating the macabre: it can be a good way to show the life-and-death seriousness of an issue.

In "Goat" (32), I took the opposite tack, that of making a point with a laugh. The humor was simple: draw a funny goat. The tricky part was to make sure we weren't poking fun at the plight of women living under repressive Islamic regimes. The real target is the husband, who is made to look like an insufferable idiot. This sparked a personal revelation of how serious commentary can underlie a lighthearted joke.

Death Worshippers* / Nov. 24, 2001

Goat / Oct. 13, 2001

Nov. 8, 2001

Dec. 7, 2001

Dec. 20, 2001

Terrorists? / Feb. 15, 2002

Gitmo PR / March 14, 2002

Truth in Advertising* / May 1, 2002

War Heads* / June 6, 2002

Comrades in Hate* / June 19, 2002

Wizard of Iran* / Aug. 14, 2002

ISRAEL

FORKUM: The first crack in the Bush Doctrine appeared just weeks after the terrorist attacks when President Bush publicly advocated a Palestinian state.[8] His apparent motive was to appease oil-producing Arab nations, most of which back Palestinian terrorism (50).

So, on the one hand, President Bush had made it perfectly clear: "Our enemy is a radical network of terrorists and every government that supports them."[1] On the other hand, he backed the creation of a government whose leaders have used terrorism for decades and made no indication they would ever do otherwise. Under the tyranny of Yasser Arafat, Palestinian territories have become factories for suicide bombers whose primary targets are Israeli civilians.[9]

Not only did Bush's advocacy of a Palestinian state practically sacrifice our ally Israel on the altar of diplomatic compromise (44), it implicitly undermined the very basis of our war against terrorists (45).

Then it got worse.

After repeated criticisms of the Israelis for using military force to fight Palestinian terrorists (46), Bush committed the even worse hypocrisy of refusing to label Arafat a terrorist [10] (48).

The Bush Doctrine was dead.

Though Bush later had harsher criticisms for Arafat (going so far as to *imply* that it was time for Arafat to go), he continued to call for a Palestinian state, seemingly oblivious to the fact that many (if not most) Palestinians wanted Israel itself gone.[11]

COX: The main thing I understand about Israel is that it's been history's perpetual scapegoat. There is literally a lot to draw upon. The tough part is to draw with a sympathetic approach while maintaining a cartoon's point and occasional humor.

"King Bush's Wisdom" (facing page) started with a biblical allusion. Allen hit upon a wonderful metaphor and it was up to me to push the emotions. There's young Israel being pulled by opposite forces—tyranny and freedom. Then there's President Bush, who obviously has the power to do justice but seems to be choosing injustice. Bush, for all his "wisdom," comes off as maniacal as Arafat. The horror of the situation is expressed by the stricken Lady Liberty. Her sorrow is *our* sorrow.

This theme was first explored by us in "With Allies Like Us..." (44). I drew the characters with a certain lightness to contrast with the dark undertones of the commentary. What I dig most about this one is the irate, dumfounded Uncle Sam. He screams with ideological indignation only to watch helplessly as a friend is thrown to the wolves. I tried to capture the wild, vile nature of rabid wolves to underscore the terrorism that has characterized militant Palestinians.

King Bush's Wisdom* / April 5, 2002

With Allies Like Us...* / Nov. 23, 2001

Nov. 23, 2001

Principle Concerns* / March 13, 2002

Escalating Violence* / March 13, 2002

Blind Diplomacy / April 4, 2002

Neo-Peaceniks* / April 12, 2002

Weighty Decision* / April 27, 2002

Help Unwanted* / June 27, 2002

Recipe for Disaster / July 15, 2002

YASSER ARAFAT

FORKUM: Palestinian leader Yasser Arafat could no longer hide behind a mask of peace, for it was "his people" who danced in the streets, gave out candy and waved "V"-for-victory signs after watching thousands die in the World Trade Center collapse. Not that we didn't know that militant Arabs hate us; we just rarely get to see it in so naked a form.[12]

Apparently sensing guilt by association, Arafat scrambled to draw a distinction between Palestinian terrorism and al Qaeda terrorism, declaring: "It must be clear that this blind terrorism [of Sept. 11] is not justified, because it targets the holy right of man to life without being part in any political conflict."[13]

Yeah, right. As if al Qaeda's goals aren't the eradication of our political system and everything we value. As if a political dispute justifies murdering innocents. Terrorism is terrorism (facing page).

Palestinian Authority officials were later caught red-handed with arms and explosives from Iran.[14] P.A.-created school books don't even show Israel on maps of "Palestine."[15] And Palestinian TV glorifies martyrdom for children[16] (57, 60). Is it any wonder why Palestinian kids become suicide murderers for Arafat's "political conflict"?

It will take more than the farce of elections (61) to create a Palestinian state where individual rights and rule of law prevail. Philosopher Leonard Peikoff observed that Iran, the world's primary source of Islamic terror, must be de-terrorized the way Germany was de-Nazified after World War II.[17]

So too with the Palestinian territories.

COX: An essential element of editorial cartoons is caricaturing "evildoers," and, personally, I find there's no one more fun to take a whack at than Yasser Arafat.

First, there's the look. Just drawing his headgear can suffice for recognition. But there's also the huge nose. And the *stubble*—my God, the vagabond, algae-looking fuzz on his large jowls is almost an icon by itself. There's the prominent lips and the bulging eyes that give the overall impression of a halibut. But that's just the obvious stuff. His face isn't who he *is*; interesting satire requires more.

"Bad Terrorism" (facing page) was our first big foray into the macabre. We weren't shooting for funny but harsh reality. Nailing his facial caricature wasn't sufficient. We needed to indicate Arafat's murderous nature. Blood-soaked hands became the symbol for his culpability. This illustration became a precursor to "Death Worshippers" and first demonstrated to me how horror can be used to drive home thought-provoking commentary.

In "Peacemaker" (58), Arafat's face wasn't even necessary. His ever-present headdress worked nicely. The tank came from a photo in a story reporting the Israelis' surrounding of Arafat's compound. The gun barrel's forced perspective was so dramatic, I immediately wanted to see Arafat peering down what looked to be the Lincoln Tunnel.

Bad Terrorism / Oct. 17, 2001

Arafat's End* / Dec. 5, 2001

Ex Libris Arafat / April 4, 2002

Peacemaker* / April 15, 2002

History Lesson / April 15, 2002

PLO Ammo / April 17, 2002

Free Elections?* / May 23, 2002

GEORGE W. BUSH

FORKUM: At first President Bush was not the target of our cartoons. I was just thankful that he, and not Al Gore, was in the White House on Sept. 11. But after Bush officially backed the creation of a Palestinian state—violating his own anti-terrorist doctrine—our gloves came off. That is why the reader will find more Bush cartoons in the Israel chapter than here.

Unfortunately, Bush has also provided us with fodder on other issues. Having inherited the "read my lips" pragmatism of his father, George W. seems to come down on the side of socialism and government expansion more often than not, from pushing to ban cloning [18] (64), to establishing protectionist import tariffs [19] (101), to spending billions on the fictitious threat of a global-warming crisis. [20]

It became difficult to tell George Bush from Al Gore (facing page).

There is a difference, however, and Bush gets some credit. He appointed the principled military mind of Donald Rumsfeld as Secretary of Defense ... though the appeasing Colin Powell almost cancels him out. Bush's "axis of evil" speech boldly labeled Iran, Iraq and North Korea as our enemies (and he later added Cuba, Libya and Syria [21]), but maybe that was just boldly stating the obvious. And there was Bush's "strike first" military policy for our enemies with the potential for developing weapons of mass destruction [22]—but isn't that the way it should be? (66)

At least we still have the Bush Doctrine ... even if he doesn't want it.

COX: Yeah, yeah ... I know. President Bush's ears aren't *that* big. And I know his eyebrows don't actually unite like two caterpillars on the make. But I must say, when you combine those characteristics with a lipless mouth and a bad haircut, you've got our Executive Chief. Sorry, Dub-Ya.

We didn't start out raking our beloved leader over the coals. After the horror of Sept. 11, we actually shied away from drawing him in a ridiculous light because he seemed to be doing the right thing. Over time, however, his contradictory nature became more apparent, so Allen's commentary and my drawing followed suit. In most of these cartoons Bush is depicted as somewhat clownish and out of his depth. But I wouldn't be surprised if his look were to change yet again. (In contrast, our Uncle Sam became what we wished President Bush would be.)

In "Compromising Positions" (facing page), I popped in for an Alfred Hitchcock-like cameo. Notice the suave, urbane gent on the right ... *c'est moi*. I haven't immortalized Allen in an editorial cartoon yet, but when the need arises for an irate protester charging the U.S. Capitol with a pen, I've got just the guy.

Compromising Positions* / June 6, 2002

Clones* / Nov. 30, 2001

Spin Control / May 20, 2002

Cold Wars: Episode II* / May 24, 2002

Push Me Pull You* / Sept. 10, 2002

LEFTISTS

FORKUM: The surge of patriotism must have initially frightened leftists, all those stars and stripes waving proudly. But it was only a matter of time.

The ruins were still smoldering in New York City when they crawled out of their caves to spew hatred for America. At a "Rally Against War & Racism" in D.C., protesters cheered as speakers compared the WTC terrorist attack to the "bomb" of AIDS, expressed solidarity with their "Palestinian brothers and sisters," and labeled America the "primary source of terrorism in the world"[23] (75).

If nothing else, leftists are adept at taking advantage of the freedoms they would deny others. They are masters of evasion, hypocrisy and lies, not unlike their comrades running socialist regimes from Cuba to "Palestine" (77).

Some examples: They claim that poverty is the primary cause of terrorism, evading the fact that Islamic tyrannies are responsible for Middle East poverty *and* terrorism[24] (73).

They claim to be champions of free speech, then *steal* newspapers containing ads advocating America's right to defend herself[25] (71).

They self-righteously posture as pacifists against violence, then protest to halt America's war against terrorism *knowing* that stopping the war would encourage more violence against Americans (facing page).

If there was ever any doubt, Sept. 11 proved that Americans and American liberty have many enemies—foreign and domestic.

COX: Caricaturing leftists with unkempt hair and flabby minds tends to be funny all by itself, but where's the "zing"? To get that, we strive to depict the danger of their ideas, not merely their looks.

In our very first editorial collaboration, "Weight of the World" (70), we didn't even bother drawing the environmentalist teacher—just his scaremongering dialogue balloon. We used the mass of Earth itself to symbolize the impossible burden of guilt being placed on little Suzies everywhere.

The first time we "burned" an American flag was in the cartoon on the facing page. I didn't enjoy drawing such a nauseating image, but the payoff was worth it: wolves in sheep suits. They captured the pathetic deception of anti-American leftists posing as "peaceful." This cartoon turned out to be a nice balance between illustrating a shameful act and lampooning the morons who are committing it.

In "Censorship, Berkeley-Style" (71), the bonfire is the star. I knew that if I could depict the book-burning convincingly, it would dramatized the irrationality of the mob.

Sept. 28, 2001

Weight of the World* / Sept. 20, 2001

Censorship, Berkeley-Style / Nov. 12, 2001

What Goes Around... / March 27, 2002

Terrorist's Charity / March 28, 2002

Judgment Call* / April 3, 2002

War Protester Check List* / April 18, 2002

State of the Arts* / May 12, 2002

White Wash* / May 15, 2002

PBS Fall / June 20, 2002

Repellent / Aug. 24, 2002

Bloodsuckers of the World* / Aug. 27, 2002

American Haters / Sept. 9, 2002

MEDIA

FORKUM: The big news *about* news in 2002: America's media have a liberal bias. Of course, this was only "news" to those liberals so blinded by their ideology that they couldn't see their own prejudices.

Take the war for example. Before the first bunker-busting bomb was dropped there were murmurs that the Taliban would be a tough enemy and Afghanistan would be the next Vietnam. The hand-wringing culminated with childish whining about the war going on for soooooo long. Then suddenly, after just a few weeks of bombing, the Taliban was defeated[26] (facing page).

Not ones to let a major victory discourage them, liberal pundits began bleating about the "quagmire" of trapping al Qaeda in mountainous regions[27] (87).

And just how large a mountain of evidence did they need to justify a preemptive strike against tyrant Saddam Hussein?[28] (86)

There was the Enron scandal, too. Democrats were looking for anything they could use to bring down President Bush's popularity. Their desperate attempts to tie Bush to Enron, and the media's credulity, were sad sights to behold[29] (85).

Of course, employing a conservative bias in reporting the news would be just as bad. Journalists need to return to objectivity, for example, calling terrorists "terrorists," which some news organizations refused to do.[30]

In the meantime, we'll just have to continue sifting the news for truth.

COX: I consider "Showdown" (facing page) one of our simplest, most effective pieces, so I'll examine it in a little more detail. Usually, Allen comes up with the initial concept for a cartoon, but I come up with some, too. Such was the case here.

First, the primary flash of an idea took hold. The word "showdown" was thrown around quite a bit by the media in the early days of the war, and it made me think of Gary Cooper, James Arness and John Wayne—actors who depicted stand-up guys out to do a bloody, thankless job with their integrity and survival on the line. I wanted Uncle Sam to be that guy. And I wanted to show how quickly he'd ended the showdown with the Taliban.

In a gunfight (as in Afghanistan), somebody dies, so I grappled with how much of the dead Taliban gunslinger needed to be seen. I figured out that simply drawing his boots pointing skyward accomplished a lot: it left plenty of room to render our valiant marshall; it minimized the death scene; and it symbolically and literally put the Taliban out of the picture.

I also wanted a funny aspect, so I put in a dopey reporter saying, "Gawd amighty! That sure wuz fast!" I faxed the drawing to Allen, and he noticed that a slight tweak of the reporter's dialogue would drive home an added point: the fact that liberal journalists have an incredible lack of confidence in our military might.

So I did a quick patch job and—Ta-daah!

Showdown* / Nov. 20, 2001

Bogeyman* / Dec. 4, 2001

Conspirators* / Jan. 17, 2002

Iraq Attack* / Feb. 15, 2002

Quagmire* / March 8, 2002

POLITICS

FORKUM: Soon after Sept. 11, members of Congress hugged and sang "God Bless America" on the Capitol steps. Then, gradually, they returned to politics as usual.

Outwardly, Democrats and Republicans seemed to continue disagreeing on many issues, such as tax cuts (91) and the relative importance of the Enron scandal[31] (92). Democrats even took control of some issues, like limiting America's access to its own oil resources, as if we weren't at war and unnecessarily dependent on oil from despotic Arab governments[32] (94).

But on closer look one sees that Republicans and Democrats often agree on a fundamental level, namely, on expanding government socialism. It turns out they are mainly arguing about matters of degree.

For instance, many Republicans and Democrats didn't argue whether to limit free speech through "campaign finance reform,"[33] they just haggled about *how much* to limit it (93).

Party lines blurred when it came to using the public's eagerness to fight the War on Terrorism as an opportunity to fund pork-barrel projects[33] (90).

And both Republicans and Democrats have used business scandals to attack capitalism and, by implication, the political and economic freedom on which our prosperity was built[34] (facing page). Bin Laden would have enjoyed that.

As with Bush and Gore, it became more and more difficult to tell Depublicans from Remocrats.

COX: One of the distinct pleasures of satirizing U.S. politics is the wealth of visual icons. Eagles, flags, monuments—they all make for a convenient shorthand when it comes to identifying the players.

The two classic symbols I really enjoy drawing are the venerable Donkey and Elephant characters. Of course, they've been drawn by hundreds of editorial cartoonists through the years, but that doesn't mean I can't make them my own.

In doing so I believe the facial anatomy doesn't need to be radically changed. The ears, eyes, nose, head shape—all should basically convey the appearance of a real animal (no Picasso am I). But those aspects can be manipulated to get across a particular persona. And sometimes they need a psychological edge to make them "breathe."

For instance, in "Bipartisan Bash" (facing page), the Democratic Donkey (or "Ass") has a manic mien. I thought of him as part John Belushi and part Mr. Haney from *Green Acres*—unstable and deceptive.

Generally, the Republican Elephant is quite different from the Donkey. I consider his character more complex. Though he's usually not eager to go along with the Donkey, his short-sighted pragmatism often gets the best of him (90, 96). I think of him as part Mr. French and part Sergeant Schultz—stately yet bumbling.

Bipartisan Bash / July 10, 2002

Cox&
Forkum

Dec. 10, 2001

Back to Normal* / Jan. 13, 2002

ENRON EVASIONS

Enron Evasions* / Jan. 24, 2002

Voice Reform* / Feb. 7, 2002

Refuge Refuse / April 24, 2002

Inciter Information / June 4, 2002

Shakedown* / Aug. 8, 2002

Bin Mates* / Aug. 24, 2002

ECONOMICS

FORKUM: From subsidizing industries at taxpayer expense [35] (100), to hampering free trade with tariffs [19] (101), to allowing envious businesses to sue better competitors (e.g., Microsoft[36]), it's clear that economic freedom in America is in jeopardy.

As philosopher Ayn Rand explained: "When government controls are introduced into a free economy, they create economic dislocations, hardships, and problems which, if the controls are not repealed, necessitate still further controls, which necessitate still further controls, etc. Thus a chain reaction is set up: the victimized groups seek redress by imposing controls on the profiteering groups, who retaliate in the same manner, on an ever-widening scale." [37]

She advocated *laissez-faire* capitalism because it "is the only social system based on the recognition of individual rights and, therefore, the only system that bans force from social relationships." [38]

This kind of rational advice is evaded by those seeking control over private enterprise. Whether it's Federal Reserve Chairman Alan Greenspan helping to wreck the economy by trying to steer it [39] (106), or Bush's corporate fraud task force threatening CEOs with jail time for their accountants' work [40] (107), the result is the same: more arbitrary government intervention and the resulting fear, loss of freedom and falling productivity.

Unless the government is returned to the principles of individual rights and economic freedom, we should expect more American corporations to shrug off involuntary servitude [41] (102).

COX: I'm not particularly knowledgeable about all his economic wizardry, but I took one look at Alan Greenspan and couldn't wait to get to my drafting table (105, 106).

As I was sketching him, I thought he looked like a mix between a battle-worn gnome and an Ivy League professor. I tried to capture the self-imposed solitude of a lore-master trapped among mere thick-headed mortals. And I found it in his eyes. For someone who purports to "see" trends before they happen, he looks remarkably blind. Those tiny eyes appear to be slits leading to a murky vault where secrets are hoarded. I like to draw his glasses as if they could magnify solar rays up to Armageddon proportions.

For all their obvious utility in economic editorial cartoons, the Bull and Bear symbols just don't have the geezer appeal that Chairman Greenspan does.

Road to Recovery* / Feb. 8, 2002

Got Subsidies?* / Dec. 18, 2001

Steal Industry / March 7, 2002

Bermuda or Bust / June 4, 2002

Future Accountability* / July 12, 2002

Enemy Blind* / July 19, 2002

Market Signals / July 25, 2002

Thus Spoke Greenspan* / July 25, 2002

Fear Factor / July 31, 2002

MISCELLANEOUS

FORKUM: In August 2001, I approached Robert Tracinski about creating editorial cartoons for his publication, *The Intellectual Activist*. He was receptive to the idea. But as excited as I was at the prospect, I took my time thinking up ideas.

Then came 9/11.

After my shock and mourning subsided, there remained a determination to fight back, particularly in the war of ideas.

The cartoon on the facing page was my and John's first war cartoon. Though never published, I still like its point: Islamic terrorists share an irrationalism with certain activists in America which results in a common bond—a willingness to use force against those who disagree, a willingness to place their causes above individual rights.

But the war wasn't the only issue.

Communist China upped military spending in a blatant threat against Taiwan's pursuit of independence[42] (112). China also supports Palestinian militants. Could it be because communists and Islamists both share the *idea* that the capitalistic West is evil?

In Africa, Zimbabwean dictator Robert Mugabe stole land from white farmers in the name of "racial justice," then gave the best farms to his cronies, all while millions of his citizens starved[43] (115). Conspicuously silent were leftists who had protested South African apartheid. Could it be because they share with Mugabe the *idea* that using government force to "rectify" racial differences is good?

The war rages on...

COX: Sometimes Allen's ideas are slightly ahead of the "hot news" curve and I end up drawing pieces that surprise me.

Until Allen offered up his Orwellian concept for "More Equal Than Others" (115), I didn't know that Zimbabwe was in the midst of such an insane, man-made food shortage.

By then I was used to illustrating the macabre, but this idea was different. The focus wasn't on the bad guy; it was on the degradation and victimization of a citizen by his own leader. It was up to me to capture the tragic absurdity of Zimbabwe's situation. Once I understood the degree of suffering that needed to be depicted, the drawing poured out of my pen.

For me, the results became another example of how cartoons can surpass laughter to approach a higher state, that of art.

Blend / Sept. 20, 2001

Bar Codes / Dec. 22, 2001

John Q* / Feb. 19, 2002

'Reunification' / March 22, 2002

The Young and the Witless / May 14, 2002

Welcome to the Club / May 30, 2002

More Equal Than Others* / June 14, 2002

New China? / Aug. 30, 2002

Peacetakers / Sept. 13, 2002

appendix:
the art of politics

This interview with Allen Forkum was originally published in The Intellectual Activist *in March 2002. It is reprinted here with permission and slightly edited from the original. References to cartoons have been updated to correspond to the pages in this book.*

TIA: How did you start doing editorial cartoons?

FORKUM: John and I have been collaborating on gag cartoons for my automotive publications for 12 years. We've admired hard-hitting editorial cartoons for many years but didn't start trying to create them until recently. Besides the sheer challenge and fun, I wanted to express opinions that I didn't see being expressed in editorial cartoons, which I find have a predominately leftist slant. John and I agreed we had something different to offer, particularly from my perspective as an Objectivist.

TIA: What prompts an idea for a cartoon? How do you develop the idea?

FORKUM: Usually a news item inspires me, but instead of firing off a letter to the editor, I'll think of a visual way to make a point. Often, it's a matter of simply exaggerating the truth, particularly a truth that's politically or philosophically evaded. Liberal and conservative politics, being a mass of contradictions, are fertile ground for humor.

In developing an idea, I'll sketch, take notes, and just turn the possibilities over in my head until an idea strikes me on an emotional level, whether serious or humorous. I use that initial reaction as a guide in developing the idea further. Once I've refined the idea, I forward it to John. I rely on him to infuse the idea with the necessary life and emotion. We go back and forth with fine-tuning until we have a final drawing.

But generally speaking, the methodology described by Ayn Rand in *The Art of Nonfiction* is the best explanation I've found for the idea-development process, e.g., choosing a subject and theme, knowing your audience, not preaching, emphasizing clarity, etc. Obviously, cartoons can't have the scope of editorials, but the process is similar.

TIA: Walk us through the process for one of your cartoons. How did you get the original idea? What prompted the specific details?

FORKUM: Soon after the War on Terrorism began, the media seemed obsessed with Attorney General Ashcroft becoming the next Hitler, because of Ashcroft's domestic security measures in response to Sept. 11. Certainly we should be concerned about protecting our civil liberties from the government, but I thought the media, particularly leftists, were blowing it out of proportion, to the point of being a distraction from our real enemy: Osama bin Laden.

How do you make that point with a cartoon?

First I wrote out the idea in word form. I noted that leftists were demonizing Ashcroft, though bin Laden was the real demon. *Demon* is obviously a strong visual, so my first sketch involved a guy drawing horns on Ashcroft's picture (see sketches on following pages).

Going further, the phrase "blowing out of proportion" reminded me of a balloon, which then reminded me of "hot air." The next sketch evolved: a "demon" Ashcroft as a huge balloon. A Statue of Liberty in his hand connotes King Kong and a threat to liberty, but as a parade balloon, it's really just hot air. One subtle but important touch was the wacky eyes, which indicate that something is fake and not really scary about the demon (see final cartoon on page 84).

On this cartoon, because it was a complex idea, John and I did a lot of fine-tuning—simplifying, clarifying, emphasizing—until we had the final. John is a great "reality check" if my ideas are too abstract, because not only does he have to "get it," he has to draw it.

Most cartoons are not that complex. For instance, "Arafat's End" (56) is based on an idea John came up with while reading an editorial that said Arafat had painted himself into a corner. After discussing possibilities for a drawing, I came up with using "terrorism" paint and an Israeli victim. Combined with John's generous use of black ink, we ended up with what I think is a serious observation about Arafat's evil ways catching up to him.

TIA: Editorial cartoons usually make their point through humor. But that often means that you are dealing with serious issues, even life-and-death issues, in a humorous way. That's a difficult line to tread. How do you do it?

FORKUM: It is difficult, but I think life-and-death issues—war, death, terrorism—issues inappropriate for humor, can sometimes carefully be used as the *context* of a humorous cartoon, as long as they are not the *object* of humor. Humor must be precisely targeted. For example, in "Showdown" (83), Uncle Sam's killing of a Taliban gunslinger—which is not funny—is used only to establish context. The humor is directed at another object, members of the press, who always seem to expect (or desire) the failure of American military justice.

Because of humor's limitations, I don't rely on it solely. Serious issues can sometimes be illustrated if a serious tone is maintained.

The "Death Worshippers" illustration (31) is not meant to be humorous. It's meant to concretize an idea evaded by the media, that militant Islam worships death. Obviously, such an illustration would not change the mind of an Islamist. But if a life-valuing person saw it, I hope they might pause and reconsider President Bush's notion that Islam had nothing to do with Sept. 11.

TIA: I've often noticed that political cartoonists say more in their cartoons than most would with words. Is the power of a political cartoon a bit like the power of high art?

FORKUM: I suppose it is a little bit, particularly in the use of drama and humor to appeal to a viewer's values and emotions. But strictly speaking, editorial cartoons have a very narrow capacity. They're great for pointing out the bad but can only imply the good—unlike high art, which can fully concretize the good. And unlike a written editorial, editorial cartoons can't make an argument. They can make an assertion, maybe draw a parallel, but that's pretty much it. And the assertion, to have any impact, still depends on the viewer's context, because there is not enough room to establish an alternate context.

Nonetheless, beyond merely entertaining, editorial cartoons can have a lot of impact. I think that power comes from the capacity to visually concretize thought-provoking ideas. Like the little boy in "The Emperor's New Clothes," an editorial cartoon can strip an idea down to its most naked, concrete form and say, "Look at this!"

If a cartoon is based on truth, it has a simplicity and directness that make its point difficult to evade, particularly for viewers whose misconceptions are targeted. For viewers whose values are affirmed, editorial cartoons can serve as a kind of emotional fuel.

It often feels like we're bombarded with absurdities. I think it's good to laugh at some of them.

Figure A: Allen's initial idea sketches

Figure B:
Allen's layout sketch

Figure C:
John's first rough sketch
(see final cartoon on
page 84)

references

Below are references to documents, news articles and editorials relating to the commentary of this book.

1. *Text: President Bush Addresses the Nation*, (*The Washington Post*, September 20, 2001) http://www.washingtonpost.com/wp-srv/nation/specials/attacked/transcripts/bushaddress_092001.html

2. *Maher Causes 'Cowardly' Flap* by Mark Armstrong (E!online, September 20, 2001) http://att.eonline.com/News/Items/0,1,8852,00.html

3. *The Powell Problem* by Robert W. Tracinski (*The Intellectual Activist*, February 1, 2002) http://www.intellectualactivist.com/php-bin/news/showArticle.php?id=61

4. *Fighting Militant Islam, Without Bias* by Daniel Pipes (*City Journal*, November 2001) http://www.danielpipes.org/article/79

5. *The Litmus Test for Authentic 'Freedom Fighters'* by Benjamin Netanyahu (*Jewish World Review*, April 19, 2002) http://www.jewishworldreview.com/0402/netanyahu.html

6. *A Culture of Death* by Robert W. Tracinski (The Ayn Rand Institute, October 15, 2001) http://www.aynrand.org/medialink/columns/rt101501.shtml

7. *In Full: Al-Qaeda Statement* (BBC, Oct. 10, 2001) http://news.bbc.co.uk/1/hi/world/middle_east/1590350.stm

8. *Bush: Palestinian State 'Part of a Vision' If Israel Respected* by Andrea Koppel and Elise Labott (CNN, October 2, 2001) http://www.cnn.com/2001/US/10/02/gen.mideast.us/

9. *Arafat's Suicide Factory* by Daniel Pipes (*New York Post*, December 9, 2001) http://www.danielpipes.org/article/89

10. *Bush Won't Label Arafat a Terrorist* by Bill Sammon (*The Washington Times*, April 2, 2002) http://www.washtimes.com/national/20020402-99688646.htm

11. *Majority of Palestinians See Israel's Elimination as Goal* (Yahoo! News, June 11, 2002) http://www.likud.nl/extr206.html

12. *Palestinian Celebrations* (HonestReporting.com, September 14, 2001) http://www.honestreporting.com/critiques/2001/68_celebrate.asp

13. *Arafat Condemns Terror Attacks* (CNN, October 10, 2001) http://fyi.cnn.com/2001/WORLD/meast/10/10/gen.qatar.arafat/

14. *Ship of Truth* by Charles Krauthammer (*The Washington Post*, January 11, 2002)
    http://www.washingtonpost.com/ac2/wp-dyn?pagename=article&node=&contentId=A28777-2002Jan10

    Arafat Takes Blame for Arms Shipment (BBC, February 14, 2002)
    http://news.bbc.co.uk/1/hi/world/middle_east/1819635.stm

15. *The Palestinian Authority School Books and Teacher's Guide* by Itamar Marcus (Center for Monitoring the Impact of Peace, March 2001) http://www.edume.org/reports/1/toc.htm

16. *Jihad for Kids* by Glenn Selig (Fox13 Investigates, February 4, 2002)
    http://www.wtvt.com/investreptr/jihad.html

    Gaza's Children Worship Martyrdom by Hamza Hendawi (Associated Press, May 14, 2002)
    http://www.recomnetwork.org/articles/02/05/14/2231215.shtml

    Palestinian TV Urging Children to Kill by David Kupelian (WorldNetDaily.com, 2001)
    http://www.frum.org/israel/ChildrentoKill.asp

    The Baby Face of Hate by David Tell (*The Weekly Standard*, June 12, 2002)
    http://www.weeklystandard.com/Utilities/printer_preview.asp?idArticle=1355&R=50842844D

17. *End States Who Sponsor Terrorism* by Leonard Peikoff (The Ayn Rand Institute, October 2, 2001)
    http://www.aynrand.org/medialink/endterrorism.shtml

18. *Bush Prods Senate to Adopt Ban on All Cloning* by Major Garrett (CNN, April 11, 2002)
    http://www.cnn.com/2002/HEALTH/04/10/bush.cloning/

    The Virtue of 'Playing God' by Alex Epstein (The Ayn Rand Institute, June 17, 2002)
    http://www.aynrand.org/medialink/virtueofplayinggod.shtml

19. *Bush Slaps Tariffs on Steel Imports* by James Cox (*USAToday*, March 6, 2002)
    http://www.usatoday.com/money/covers/2002-03-06-steel.htm

20. *Bush Dismisses Administration's Climate Change Study* by John Heilprin (*Nando Times*, June 4, 2002)
    http://www.nandotimes.com/politics/story/424128p-3385085c.html

    Global Warming vs. Science by Robert W. Tracinski (The Ayn Rand Institute, December 1997)
    http://www.aynrand.org/medialink/warming.html

21. *US Expands 'Axis of Evil'* (BBC, May 6, 2002)
    http://news.bbc.co.uk/1/hi/world/americas/1971852.stm

22. *'Strike First' to Become Formal U.S. Policy* (Fox News, June 10, 2002)
http://www.foxnews.com/story/0,2933,54918,00.html

23. *Rally Against War & Racism* (C-SPAN, September 29, 2001)
Some quotes collected at anti-war activists' Web site:
http://www.iacenter.org/s29_quotes.htm

24. *World Leaders Say Poverty Breeds Terrorism* by Traci Carl, AP (*North County Times*, March 22, 2002)
http://www.nctimes.net/news/2002/20020322/55837.html

   The Root Cause of Terrorism by Benjamin Netanyahu (*The Wall Street Journal*, April 19, 2002)
http://www.opinionjournal.com/editorial/feature.html?id=105001950

   God and Mammon: Does Poverty Cause Militant Islam? by Daniel Pipes (*The National Interest*, Winter 2002) http://www.danielpipes.org/article/104

25. *Berkeley Leftists vs. Free Speech* (The Ayn Rand Institute, October 25, 2001)
http://www.aynrand.org/medialink/pr102501.shtml

26. *U.S. Chases Fleeing Taliban Troops* (NewsMax.com Wires, November 14, 2001)
http://www.newsmax.com/archives/articles/2001/11/13/165333.shtml

27. *The Prophets of Defeatism* by Robert W. Tracinski (*The Intellectual Activist*, March 8, 2002)
http://www.intellectualactivist.com/php-bin/news/showArticle.php?id=114

28. *Saddam's Rap Sheet* by Daniel Pipes and Jonathan Schanzer (*New York Post*, August 20, 2002)
http://www.danielpipes.org/article/444

29. *Liberal Conspiracy Theories* by Robert W. Tracinski (*The Intellectual Activist*, January 18, 2002)
http://www.intellectualactivist.com/php-bin/news/showArticle.php?id=51

30. *'Terrorist' Term Scrubbed by Minnesota Paper* by Jennifer Harper (*The Washington Times*, April 4, 2002)
http://www.washtimes.com/national/20020404-5562528.htm

31. *Enron Ethics* by Robert W. Tracinski (*The Intellectual Activist*, January 25, 2002)
http://www.intellectualactivist.com/php-bin/news/showArticle.php?id=59

32. *Nine out of Ten Caribou Support Drilling* by Ann Coulter (TownHall.com, April 18, 2002)
http://www.townhall.com/columnists/anncoulter/ac20020418.shtml

33. *Campaign Finances and Corruption* by Robert W. Tracinski (*The Intellectual Activist*, March 22, 2002)
http://www.intellectualactivist.com/php-bin/news/showArticle.php?id=129

34. *The War on CEOs* by Robert W. Tracinski (*The Intellectual Activist*, July 12, 2002)
http://www.intellectualactivist.com/php-bin/news/showArticle.php?id=264

35. *Senate Raises Farm Subsidies* by Dave Boyer (*The Washington Times*, May 9, 2002)
http://www.washtimes.com/national/20020509-618800.htm

36. *Drop the Antitrust Case Against Microsoft* by Onkar Ghate (The Ayn Rand Institute, March 6, 2002)
http://www.aynrand.org/medialink/freemicrosoft.shtml

37. *Stalinism Is the Only Victor in Cold War* by Ayn Rand (*Los Angeles Times*, July 22, 1962)
From book: *The Ayn Rand Lexicon* edited by Harry Binswanger (Meridian, 1986)

38. *The New Fascism: Rule by Consensus* by Ayn Rand (1966)
From book: *Capitalism: The Unknown Ideal* by Ayn Rand (New American Library, 1986)

39. *Capitalists vs. Crooks* by Elan Journo (The Ayn Rand Institute, July 22, 2002)
http://www.aynrand.org/medialink/greedisgood.shtml

    Rational Pessimism by Richard Salsman (CaptialismMagazine.com, June 12, 2002)
http://www.capitalismmagazine.com/2002/june/rs_pessimism.htm

40. *Bush Signs Corporate Fraud Bill* (NewsMax.com Wires, July 31, 2002)
http://www.newsmax.com/archives/articles/2002/7/30/142310.shtml

41. *NY Times Takes Aim at 'Greedy' Executives* by Mike Godfrey (Tax-News.com, May 27, 2002)
http://www.tax-news.com/asp/story/story.asp?storyname=8303

42. *China Ups Military Spending* (BBC, March 6, 2002)
http://news.bbc.co.uk/1/hi/world/asia-pacific/667352.stm

43. *The Post-Colonialist Famine* by Robert W. Tracinski (*The Intellectual Activist*, June 14, 2002)
http://www.intellectualactivist.com/php-bin/news/showArticle.php?id=235

about the
authors

Allen Forkum is co-owner and art director
of AutoGraphic Publishing Company in
Nashville, Tenn.

John Cox is an illustrator, cartoonist and fine
artist. He exhibits his paintings at the Abstein
Gallery in Atlanta, Ga.